50 THINGS YOU CAN DO TO SAVE THE WORLD

FOR YOUNG READERS

Dedicated to each and every eco-warrior,
wherever in the world you are.
—Kim

Racehorse for Young Readers books may be purchased in bulk at special discounts for sales promotion, corporate gifts, fund-raising, or educational purposes. Special editions can also be created to specifications. For details, contact the Special Sales Department, Skyhorse Publishing, 307 West 36th Street, 11th Floor, New York, NY 10018 or info@skyhorsepublishing.com.

Racehorse for Young Readers™ is a pending trademark of Skyhorse Publishing, Inc.®, a Delaware corporation.

Visit our website at www.skyhorsepublishing.com.

10 9 8 7 6 5 4 3 2 1

Library of Congress Cataloging-in-Publication Data is available on file.

Production by Madeleine Ehm
Editorial by Sam Hutchinson
Design by Kim Hankinson
Cover design by Vicky Barker

Print ISBN 978-1-63158-622-4
E-Book ISBN: 978-1-63158-623-1

Printed in China

Activities for ...

... bold, brave, green heroes,
caring, daring, dreaming, mindful,
shouting, creative, rescuing,
resourceful, EARTH—WARRIORS!

KIM HANKINSON

HOW TO
SAVE THE WORLD

This book is full of activities
to try to help save the world.

Earth is one pretty special place. As far as we know
it is the only place like it in the whole universe!
Steadily, the number of people who live on our planet
has been going up, as has our love of stuff! Every
day we take more resources from our wonderful
planet and create lots of waste too.

So what can we do?

We can start small. The ways in which we live always
have an impact on our planet, so even small choices
we make can make a big difference.

Then there are the big battles to fight—**climate
change**, rising sea levels, pollution, deforestation, loss
of wildlife—for this we need some people power!

LET'S DO THIS!

CONTENTS & ACTIVITY CHECKLIST:

ACTIVITY KEY

RECYCLE	SHOUT	THINK	MAKE	NATURE	CAREFUL!

Always ask an adult when you see a red warning symbol!

Share a ride!

Traveling together is much kinder to the environment. Less polluting gases are released per person when many people travel together—buses and trains are great and full cars are better too.

The kit

Every eco-activist needs a toolkit!

LEFTOVER CARDSTOCK & PAPER

HOMEMADE NOTEPAD FOR BIG IDEAS

GARDEN TOOLS

FABRIC GLUE & PAINT

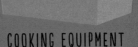

COOKING EQUIPMENT

SEWING KIT

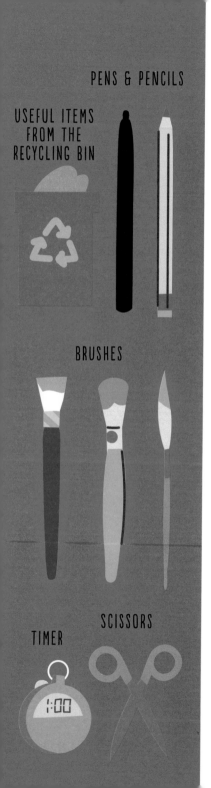

USEFUL ITEMS
FROM THE
RECYCLING BIN

PENS & PENCILS

BRUSHES

TIMER

SCISSORS

Key words

You'll find these
key words in bold
throughout the book.

POLLUTER
A person or thing that adds poisonous or
harmful substances to the environment.

POLLINATOR
An animal that takes pollen from one
flowering plant to another. This is how
plants reproduce.

OXYGENATING
Adds the gas oxygen, which is what
humans need to breath, to something
such as air or water.

CLIMATE CHANGE
A natural process where the usual weather
in a place changes over time—sped up to
dangerous levels by human activity.

MIGRATION
Moving from one place in the world
to another.

REFUGEE
A person who has had to leave their
home to escape from war, persecution,
natural disaster, or climate change.

LANDFILL
Where waste is buried in the ground.

Daily dares

Mix and pick these do-good tips!

Copy these ideas on to scraps of paper and pop them into a used jar. Whenever you are bored, or feeling worried about the planet, take one out and do something to help. You can also add new ideas whenever you think of them, so you will never forget your GENIUS ideas for saving the world one action at a time. The more you do them, the more you help. Now that is genius.

GO ELECTRICITY FREE TODAY

COLLECT HELPFUL IDEAS FROM OTHER PAGES OF THIS BOOK

BUY LOCAL!

REPAIR OLD ELECTRONICS

GIVE & SHOP SECOND-HAND

SAY NO TO A LIFT
AND WALK

MAKE FOOD
TO SHARE

SIGN A PETITION
THAT HELPS THE WORLD

PLANT A TREE

TURN DOWN THE HEAT

GO PLASTIC-FREE TODAY

LITTER PICK!

MEAT-FREE DAY

VOLUNTEER

Having an impact

Ask questions, think differently!

Buying new stuff we do not need or only use once creates A LOT of waste. One of the best things we can do for the planet is not buying things we do not really need. Your choices are more powerful than you know!

WHAT IS IT MADE OF?

Find out where the materials in your products come from and are made.

WHERE IN THE WORLD?

Are things made where laws protect the people and the environment?

UPGRADE?

An upgrade means you replace something with a newer version. Do you think that we need to upgrade when something still works?

PACKAGING

If you order online, does the product come wrapped in too much stuff?

PRODUCTION

Every piece of plastic that ever existed STILL exists, even if it is recycled into something else!

Creating new products can be very polluting, harming people and animals too. Can you buy it second-hand instead?

TRANSPORT

WASTE

Will you get enough use out of it? Can it be recycled or fixed if it breaks, or will it go to landfill?

How do things reach you? Would buying locally-made items and food that is in season reduce fuel use?

VOTE WITH YOUR FEET

Pop on your favorite slippers and watch your favorite movie. Leave it a week and be a lazy shopper. You might change your mind and help the planet!

Catwalk-ing

Fast fashion and wearing something only once is a big **polluter**. Instead of buying something new, try this patching fix!

REUSE OR BORROW THESE:

Natural felt (reused)
Pencil
Scissors
Needle
Thread
Safety pin
Fabric glue

1. Mark out the design on natural felt. Cut the main shape out.

2. Sew in details. Do not worry if the back is messy!

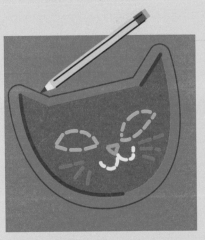

3. Place your design on another piece of felt and draw around it leaving some space.

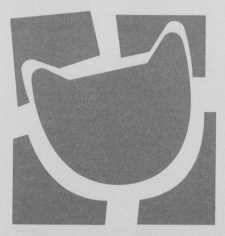

4. Cut out the larger shape on your second piece of felt.

5. Sew on a safety pin leaving the opening side free.

COVER A STAIN

6. Use fabric glue to stick your design to backing with pin. Wear with pride!

In 2019, Extinction Rebellion started the #boycottfashion #XR52 week challenge. Could you go for a whole year without buying new clothes?

PATCH A RIP
Skip step 6 and sew on directly to make an awesome patch fix.

FREEDOM

Letters are great, too!

Plant power

Eat it, grow it, never throw it!

Magic lettuce

Cut the base of a lettuce off and eat the leaves. Put the base in a water dish and watch it re-grow!

Re-rooting Specimens!

You can grow loads of herbs like basil and mint from parts of the main plant. Cut a stalk from the stem, a little distance below where the leaves are growing. Remove all of the leaves from the bottom half. Pop in water for a week, then simply pop in the soil. Weirdly wonderful!

Look! New roots!

NOT SO SCRAPPY

All you need is some potato peel that has a few eyes on it. Dry it overnight and then just plant it eye-side up. You will have a new potato plant shoot in less than a week!

EYE

Each year, 88 million tons of food are wasted in the EU alone!

SAY HELLO CELERY!

Cut off the bottom 2 in. of the stalk. Put the celery stalks you will be eating now in water and they will stay fresh. Put the base in water (just like with the lettuce) and once it begins to grow, plant in soil and wait for it to be as big as it was the last time!

Power shower

Beat the clock with a
two-minute shower.

1. Use something to time
   yourself, ideally a
   borrowed waterproof
   timer—set to two minutes.

Cut down from a ten-
minute to a two-minute
shower and over the
course of a year you
will have saved about
2,500 gallons. That's
the same as 10,000
water bottles!

2. Start the shower and get the
   temperature right, collecting the
   water in a bucket for washing up or
   watering plants. Don't go too hot,
   as this takes longer to heat up!

This is not an excuse not to wash your hands after using the toilet or brushing your teeth! You still need to do that!

4. When the timer chimes, turn off the water and get dry, feeling clean and extra good about doing your bit for the environment.

At home, showers are believed to be the third largest use of water after toilets and washing machines

3. Ready... set... start the timer and... WASH! Start at your head and finish with your toes.

Insect rescue

Plant local wildflowers and help support the bees.

SCATTER WILDFLOWER SEEDS

CREATE A BEE CORRIDOR

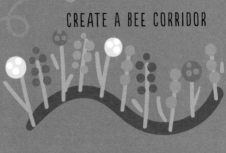

NO CHEMICAL
WEED KILLERS!

KEEP A LITTLE PILE
OF DEADWOOD AND
LEAVES FOR BEETLES

MAKE A WATER FEATURE

Pollinating insects like bees help our flowering plants reproduce. Without them our food chains would collapse, so those little creatures make a big difference!

SEED SCATTER

How to reclaim an unloved area of dirt by scattering wildflower seeds to help pollinators, like bees.

In cities like London, man-made, mile-long "Bee Corridors" help pollinators and other insects survive and even thrive.

1. Choose wildflower seeds that would grow in your area. Avoid imported plant species and plant at the right time of year

2. Choose a bare patch and use a garden fork to loosen the top layer of soil a bit.

3. Scatter plenty of the wildflower seeds onto the soil and sprinkle on a little water. Add a marker so you remember where they are.

4. Keep them watered (but do not drown them) and watch them grow!

Organize!

Join an environmental activity or event in your area, or start one yourself!

"BEE" A COMMUNITY

Ask neighbors and friends to help you create a bee corridor by planting more wildflowers for **pollinators**. See page 18 for tips!

LITTER PICKING

Join a beach clean-up or a litter picking event in your area.

REPAIR CAFE

Organize a party where your friends and their families swap skills. Can you help someone fix something?

A company in Nairobi creates amazing animal sculptures from discarded flip-flops washed up on beaches in Kenya. So far they have recycled over a million flip-flops.

PROTEST

Although we can make a difference on our own, people power can have an impact on businesses and governments, bringing attention to an issue you care about. Have a big idea? Ask your school if they can help bring it to life.

PLANT TREES

Plant **oxygenating**, ground-holding, life-supporting trees together. They take a long time to grow, so let's get started!

CITIZEN SCIENCE

People all over the world use online surveys to help conservationists watch over wildlife.

Fancy dresser

Most dress-up costumes are made of plastic fabric and only last a few wears! Why not create your own and steal the show, not the planet?

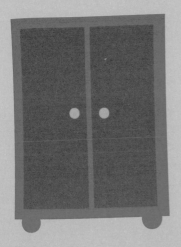

1. Look at what you have

(A green top could be used for a turtle, dinosaur, plant or superhero costume.)

2. Make Ideas

Look online, in shops, books and magazines. Look at what you have, would anything work?

3. Get crafty!

Draw and cut out props on paper or cardboard and color with paints and felt-tip pens. You can use and adapt props you have at home. Try face paints too!

SUPERHERO

QUEEN

LION KING!

PIRATE AND PARROT

WITCH AND CAT

ARTIST

ANCIENT GREEK
WITH HARP

DAY OF THE
DEAD SKULL

ROBOT

CHALLENGE!

Look at the ideas for costumes above.
Can you use this top for any of them?
Can you think of more ideas they
could be used for?

The MEAT-FREE challenge!

Cut down on your meaty meals and save the world one salad at a time!

COLOR CHALLENGE

Create your own meat-free sandwich. Include food of every color of the rainbow!

Farming animals for meat is a big contributor to **climate change**. Reducing meat consumption is healthy for you and the planet.

WASH IT FIRST!

Locally grown, seasonal food is kind to the environment.

Animal hero

Look out for local and international wildlife.
Start in your own garden or park by helping
birds find food and water, especially in winter.

**REUSE OR
BORROW THESE:**

Big and small plastic bottle
(reused or from recycling)

Scissors

Garden cane or similar

Electrical tape

Birdseed

String

1. Use bottles from the recycling bin.
   Remove the lid of the larger bottle. Pierce
   a hole and carefully cut away a large
   section of one side leaving a height of
   around 1 in. from the base. Avoid cutting
   near the top.

Some birds fly
thousands of miles every
year during **migration**,
visiting places all over the
world. Helping birds in your
back garden could have a
GLOBAL impact!

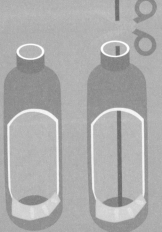

2. Stick some
   electrical tape at
   the bottom. Place
   the garden cane
   inside the bottle
   and cut it at
   the top.

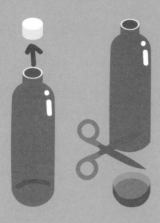

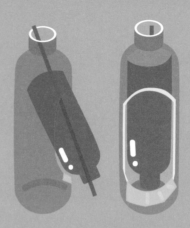

3. Remove the lid on the smaller bottle and cut off the base.

4. Slide the smaller bottle upside down onto the garden cane in the large bottle through the hole in the side, and place it all the way inside.

5. Use a funnel to pour birdseed into the top. It will land inside the small bottle.

6. Place some string over the top, twist the cap back on over it.

7. Hang from somewhere the cat cannot reach!

Paper partying!

Single-use plastic is very wasteful and a lot of it ends up in our oceans. Avoid plastic party poopers with this easy paper craft!

1. Fold the edge of some A4 paper over about 0.75 in.

2. Turn the paper over.

3. Fold the same side by the same width.

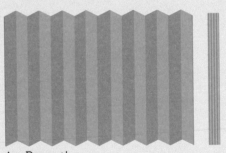

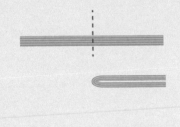

4. Repeat!

5. When you have a neat strip of folded paper, fold it in half.

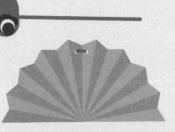

6. Attach the sides that meet in the middle with string.

7. Cut out paper features and get creative!

BUNTING

Join single pieces like this to create amazing bunting!

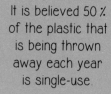

It is believed 50 % of the plastic that is being thrown away each year is single-use.

PRETTY WRAPPING

Join two pieces to make a circle.

We produce about 30 % more waste during clebrations like Christmas.

Paint paper and let it dry for awesome experiments like this watermelon!

CUTE CHARACTERS

REUSE

Accordions are easy to flatten and pack away for you next party.

PARTY CUP POP-OUTS

LOOK, no straws!

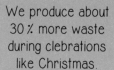

29

Make a megaphone!

Get your voice heard! Create your own megaphone and spread the word about saving the world.

REUSE OR BORROW THESE:
Large reused construction paper
Two pencils   Scissors
Tape   String   Ruler

1. On a flat surface, tack the edges of the construction paper with tape.

2. Tie two pencils together with string longer than the paper. Place one eraser end down, about 4 in. from the edge of your paper.

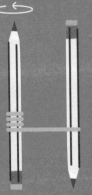

3. Twist the pencil until the loose pencil touches the furthest edge of the paper. Using your eraser end down pencil as an anchor, draw a curve with the other pencil.

4. Now twist the pencil again making the string much shorter.

5. When the pencil is about 1 in. away from the edge but still in the middle widthways, draw a second arch.

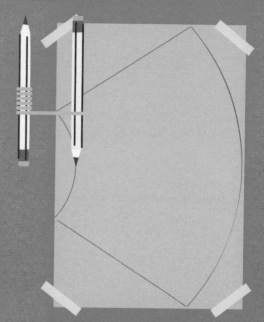

6. Cut out the shape.

7. Cut a strip of paper for the handle.

8. Stick the strip down at each end with enough room for your hand underneath.

9. Create a cone, overlapping the edges and taping it in place both inside and outside.

SPEAK UP!

10. Decorate, hold, shout and get your voice heard!

Make a statement!

Wear your message with you wherever you go with this upcycled "bag for life."

1. Choose an old top you were going to throw out; perhaps it is tatty or stained. Turn it inside out and lay flat. If you are using a tank, skip to step 3.

2. Draw lines in chalk, as shown. Cut along the lines through the whole T-shirt with a good pair of scissors.

3. Snip the base into little strips and then tie them tightly in double knots, front to back.

4. Turn the T-shirt bag inside out again so now it is the right way around. All the knots will be hidden inside the bag.

5. Create a stencil: Draw a design on a piece of paper. Color it in. Cut away the areas you have colored in or any shapes that are part of your design.

6. Using a flat-end brush, paint the design on using fabric paint. Always draw your brush from the stencil first to avoid blobbing.

7. Allow to dry and ...

ROCK THAT BAG!

SKOLSTREJK FÖR KLIMATET

In late August 2018, Greta Thunberg sat alone outside Parliament with a sign. Her words, translated as SCHOOL STRIKE FOR CLIMATE, kicked off school children's strikes across the world demanding action to prevent further climate change.

Precious water

Water is a finite resource and one of the things all animals (including humans) need to live! How can you find fresh water to drink?

REUSE OR BORROW THESE:

Big mixing bowl
Mud
Warm water
A small jar or glass, shorter than the mixing bowl
Half of a plastic bag
A penny or marble

1. Put some mud from outside into to a mixing bowl and mix with warm water.

2. Put a short glass or used jar into the mixture in the middle of the bowl.

3. Stretch the plastic bag over the top, sealing the sides tightly. The bag needs to be neat but with a little slack.

4. Gently place the penny in the middle of the bag, above your glass or jar.

5. Place on a sunny spot. Check an hour later. Any water in the glass should be clean.

WHAT HAPPENS WHEN THERE'S NO WATER?

Scarcity of water pushes people into conflict and sometimes people have to leave their homes and countries as environmental **refugees.** It is hard to make more freshwater, so what can we do?

Wangari Maathai was awarded the Nobel Peace prize for her work with women in Africa. What did Wangari and the women do to save their home and keep safety and peace? They planted trees!

PLANT TREES!
Tree roots help absorb water into the ground and keep it there. Otherwise heavy rain can cause floods and even landslides.

BE AWARE
Some farming/production practices poison water or even divert it away from people who need it, especially in poorer countries. We can be aware of what we buy and where it is made. Make smart choices!

GO GREENER!
Climate change is reducing rainfall in large parts of the world like Northern Africa and increasing it in others. Try to cut down on waste.

Ever wondered why the sea will not help us in a water shortage? Did you know that salt makes your body want to vomit water? Seawater contains so much salt that if you could drink some, you would pee more liquid than you had drunk!

Bananas waste!

Like most foods, the world's most popular fruit often ends up in our trashcans. Try this banana-gone-bad-but-still-good recipe!

YOU WILL NEED

3 very ripe bananas
2 oz. butter, softened and cubed
1 egg
7 oz. plain flour
7 oz. caster sugar
1 teaspoon baking soda

OPTIONAL

Cinnamon, ginger, vanilla essence

Oven preheated to 356°F (180°C)

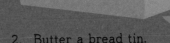

2. Butter a bread tin.

3. In a bowl mash up your bananas until they are really gooey.

1. Preheat your oven to 356°F (180°C).

Make sure you do not throw away food too early and only buy what you know you will need.

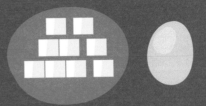

CAREFUL! HOT CAKE! USE OVEN MITTS!

4. Add in the butter and egg, then beat well.

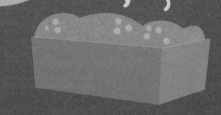

In Britain, it is estimated 1.4 million bananas go in the bin every day! Every single banana is imported so that is a lot of wasted fuel.

5. Now add the flour, sugar, baking soda and a teaspoon of a spice you like.

8. Poke through it with a knife. The knife will come out clean if it is ready. If not, cook for longer.

6. Mix until it is smooth.

9. Leave the bread to rest in the pan for ten minutes, then turn out onto a drying rack to cool down.

10. Eat, share, and spread the news about banana waste!

7. Pour the batter into a bread tin and bake for 50 minutes.

Get gifted

Show some love without creating more waste by giving a gift that will never end up in the trash!

Recycle with collage and design your own card.

YOUR FAVE BAND
ADMITS 1

TICKETS

Can you find a day out that would be the perfect treat? Then make memories, not waste.

SKILLS

Share your talent and teach someone a new skill.

TIME

Give someone your time! Helping in the garden or with a meal seems like a small thing but it can mean a lot to someone.

ANIMAL MAGIC!

Maybe you would like to sponsor an animal or make a donation to help an endangered species?

There are lots of charities helping look after animals and their habitats. This can make a really nice present for someone who loves animals.

Otherwise, you could make something inspired by their favorite animal, like an epic poster collage made from magazines and drawings.

IN the UK, about £42 million unwanted Christmas presents are thrown out in **landfills** each year!

Get creative and be different!

Do not bottle it

Make planet-friendly drinks! Ditch single-use cartons or bottles for a customized reusable bottle.

REUSE OR BORROW:

Glass bottle	Scissors
Felt scraps	Fabric glue
Pins	Needle
Felt-tip pen	Thread

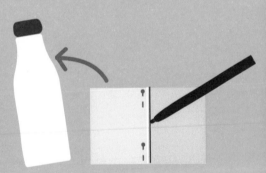

1. Lay your bottle over the felt. The felt must be wide enough to wrap all around it with some to spare.

2. Pin the felt together around the bottle. Remove the bottle and mark where the felt meets with a felt-tip pen.

3. Unpin and mark between the line you have drawn and the other end. Draw some shapes and cut them out.

4. Turn the felt over so you cannot see the pen lines. Stick it on to a piece of felt of a contrasting color using fabric glue. Allow to dry.

5. Wrap the felts around the bottle so you can see your shapes. Pin in place.

6. Stitch where the felts meet and cut any excess felt off.

Art power

Many plastics are in fact non-recyclable.
Make a protest sculpture made from plastic waste.

Only 9 % of new plastic worldwide is recycled.

1. Collect and clean the non-recylable packaging that would normally go in the trash. Lay it all out in front of you.

2. Stack and stick the plastic together using finer bits of plastic, creating your own unique sculpture. Add detail with felt-tip pens.

JELLYFISH

Plastic bags make excellent jellyfish. Try hanging them on strings and shredding a second one as long tentacles.

FANS AND PLATES

Draw branches and patterns on single-use plates and other flat objects to create fan and plate coral.

OCEANIC IDEAS

You might pick a theme to help you. Try these recycled reef creations.

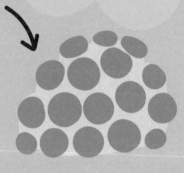

BUILD REEFS

Try sticking lots of single-use cups together to make tubular coral.

The "Great Pacific Garbage Patch" is one of five trash islands floating in our oceans. It is three times the size of France and getting bigger.

3. Exhibit in your front room window at home with a sign, or at school or in a public space—with permission.

4. Photograph the sculpture and write a letter to your mayor or government official.

FLY RIGHT!

Ever seen a tail that talks?
Spread the word with this recycled kite.

REUSE OR BORROW:

Sticks from a garden or
   local park
Scissors
Old plastic bags
Sticky tape
Toilet paper tube
String or thread

Try a thicker
plastic bag
for an extra
tough kite!

1. Cut the lightweight skewers
   or sticks so that one is an
   extra half longer than the other.
   So if the short stick is 8 in., the
   long one will be 12 in.

2. Open up a plastic bag and lay it flat.

3. Make a cross shape with your supports
   and stick them to the bag with tape.

4. Create your handle. Cut a toilet roll tube lengthways and then roll it tight. Stick it back with tape.

5. Tape the end of the string to the handle and roll plenty of string on to your newly made handle.

For the string to connect the kite, you can use lots of things like fishing line, sewing cotton, or nylon thread. Just make sure it's light and strong.

6. Cut about 6 in. of string and tie each end to the horizontal rod with double knots, as shown.

7. Make a tail from another plastic bag in a different color.

8. Cut lettering out of the remaining bag and stick to the tail. Decorate the kite and spread the word.

Many cities and countries are now banning or charging for plastic bags. Ireland alone found charging for bags meant 90 % fewer were used!

PASS IT ON

There is no need to throw away things you do not want. Here are just some of the ways we can pass on before we recycle!

BOOKS

You can donate books, or pass ones you have enjoyed to friends.

CLOTHES & SHOES

Organize a clothes swap with your friends! If there is something left you can donate to charity or second-hand shops.

ELECTRONICS

You can pass on MP3 players or video games to shops who sell them second-hand. You might even get some money back!

GLASSES

Charities recycle glasses by passing them onto people in poorer communities.

JUST ABOUT ANYTHING

If you are not sure where to donate things, try selling or advertising them online!

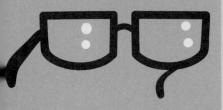

RECYCLE

These things are all recycled. Can you recycle anything else?

PAPER & CARDBOARD

GLASS

CLOTHES

ELECTRONICS

LIGHTBULBS

PLASTIC CONTAINERS

PRINTER INK

PLASTIC BAGS

FOIL

BATTERIES

Recycling is great but it is better if you can reduce what you consume and then reuse what you have. Remember, in this order: Reduce, reuse, recycle!

"I thought I couldn't make a difference because I was too small."
—Greta Thunberg

"What you do makes a difference, and you have to decide what kind of difference you want to make."
—Jane Goodall

"It's the little things that citizens do. That's what will make the difference. My little thing is planting trees."
—Wangari Maathai